HEY, LOOK AT ME!

I LIKE TO PLAY

A Book For Boys

MERRY THOMASSON
Illustrated by G.B. McIntosh

I can do it. You will see.
Turn the page and look at me.

MERRYBOOKS • CHARLOTTESVILLE, VIRGINIA

Batter up! Hey, look at me playing baseball. Strike one! I must watch the ball and swing hard. Crack! I hit it and run to first base as fast as I can. I sometimes strike out, but I always keep trying. Some day I hope to hit a home run. I will race around all three bases and then to home plate without stopping. I can do it!

Take your mark, get set, go! Hey, look at me running to win the race. I jump over hurdles as fast as I can. Other runners are close behind. I push myself to run my best race every time. It makes me feel good when I try my hardest. I can do it!

Hey, look at me dribbling the ball up the court. I am a basketball player. Players on the other team are trying to steal the ball from me. I throw it to my teammates. They pass it back to me, and I shoot the ball through the hoop. Basketball is a very fast game. I play by the rules and play hard. I can do it!

Hey, look at me! I am racing through the water. I kick my legs and pull with my arms. I use all my muscles when I swim, so it makes me strong. I like to jump into the pool and do the side stroke, the breast stroke, and the backstroke. I can even swim under the water. Sometimes I just float on my back and look up at the sky. If I keep at it, I will become a good swimmer. I can do it!

Hey, look at me! I am playing golf. I tee up my golf ball and hit it down the fairway. I keep my eye on the ball as I swing. When the ball is on the smooth, grassy circle called a green, I tap it with my putter into the hole. It is fun to spend the day outside playing golf. To play well, I must concentrate and hit the ball just right. I can do it!

Down, set, hike! Hey, look at me! I am running with the football. My teammates help by blocking the other team's players so that they cannot tackle me. I try to score a touchdown. I practice running and passing and catching the ball. It takes teamwork to win the game, and it is fun to be part of a team. I can do it!

Hey, look at me on the pommel horse. I am a gymnast. I also swing myself on the rings and the parallel bars. When I tumble, I do handsprings and flips. Gymnastics makes me flexible and strong. With time and practice, I learn to make each movement perfect. It is not easy. But I can do it!

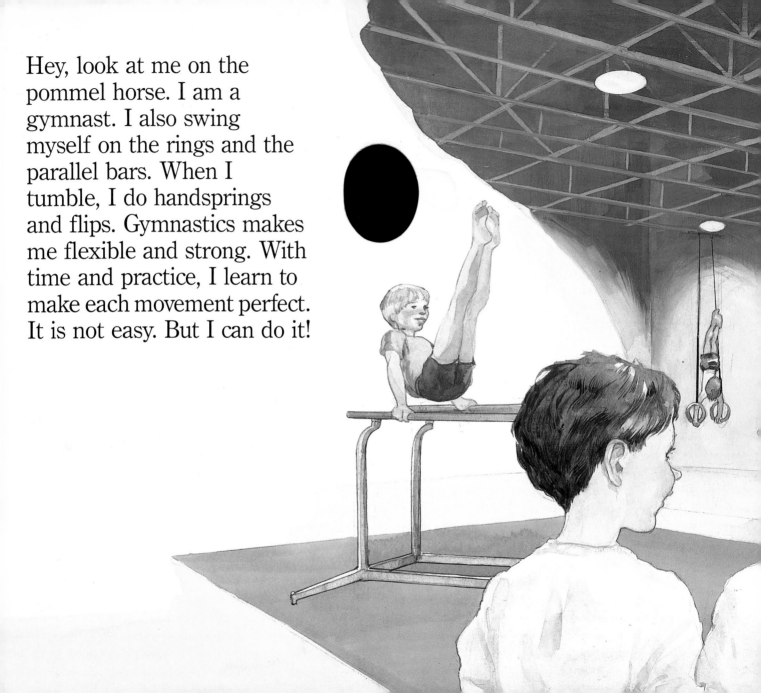

Hey, look at me! I am a tennis player. I hit the ball across the net with a swing of my racket. The tennis ball travels very fast, so I move quickly, too. I keep my eye on the ball at all times. It is fun and the more I play, the better I become. I can do it!

Hey, look at me playing soccer. My teammates and I kick the ball to each other as we run down the field. I can use any part of my body except my arms and hands. Hurray! Our team scores a point when we kick the ball past the goalie into the net. Everyone on the team is important. Sometimes we win, and sometimes we lose, but we always have lots of fun. I can do it!

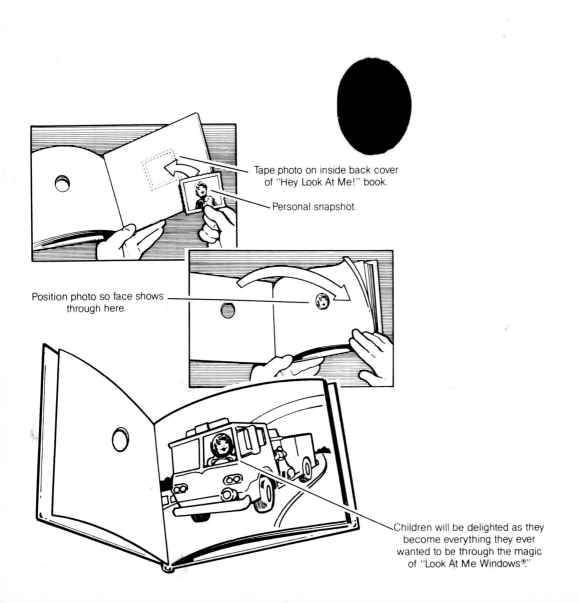

Tape photo on inside back cover
of "Hey Look At Me!" book.

Personal snapshot.

Position photo so face shows
through here.

Children will be delighted as they
become everything they ever
wanted to be through the magic
of "Look At Me Windows®."